INSTEAD OF

INSTEAD OF A MASS

ELIZABETH BARTLETT

HEADLAND

© Elizabeth Bartlett 1991

All rights reserved

British Library Cataloguing in Publication Data
Bartlett, Elizabeth, *1924-*
Instead of a mass.
I. Title
821.914

ISBN 0 907034 58 3

First published in 1991 by HEADLAND PUBLICATIONS
NORTH WALES & WIRRAL

Editorial Address:
Tŷ Coch, Galltegfa, Llanfwrog, Ruthin, Clwyd LL15 2AR

Sales and Distribution:
38 York Avenue, West Kirby, Wirral, Merseyside L48 3JF

Cover photograph by Denis Perkins: 11th century wallpainting on the chancel arch, Coombes Church, West Sussex. A note in the church refers to it as an 'Atlas figure. . . perhaps in allusion to the scene in Prudentius's *Psychomachia*, the Building of the Temple of the Soul.'

Printed and bound by Gee & Son Ltd., Denbigh, Clwyd, Wales

David

Fröhliche Weinachten, 1993

Elizabeth

To
PROFESSOR BRUCE MARTIN

CONTENTS

	page
HAND TO MOUTH	9
IN THE LYRICAL TRADITION	10
EGO TRIP	11
SMALL DOLE	12
TOO MUCH ANGST	13
MUNICIPAL IKEBANA	14
EARLY SORROW	15
ALPHABET BOARD	16
DE PROFUNDIS	17
YOU TOUCHED ME	18
A PERILOUS ZONE	19
AN IDEAL FAMILY	20
LETTING GO	21
A STRAW MAT	22
TEA WITH COPERNICUS AND WAFFLES	23
DRINKING WITH HENRY	25
REDEMPTION	26
VERY SAMUEL	27
FORM	28
ASSAULT AND BATTERY	29
THE JOKE SHOP	30
THIS ROOM	31
THE BRADFORD CONNECTION	32
A TRANSLATION	33
THE NOVELIST	34

EDWARD THOMAS AT SURINDERS	35
MODEL T.	36
A GENETIC ERROR	37
IRISH HAIR	38
MRS DESECRATE'S BABY BOY	40
THE EIGHT-FOLD WAY	41
IMAGO 1943	42
TRIPTYCH	43
FIGHT OR FLIGHT	45
FROM THIS DAY ON	46
SOLOMON'S SEAL	47
READING IN CAMBRIDGE	48
NUDE DECLINING	49
SMILE FOR DADDY	50
THIN ICE	51
BAROQUE NIGHTS AND NATURALISTIC DAYS	52
MR ZWEIGENTHAL	53
GOODSFIELD	54
THEATRE IN THE ROUND	55
PER FUMUM	56
SPANISH MOSS	57
THE CAVE YOU WOULD NOT ENTER	58
KIM'S GAME	59
THE NUCLEAR GIRLS	60

ACKNOWLEDGEMENTS

Acknowledgements are due to the magazines, journals and anthologies in which some of these poems first appeared:
Ambit, The Cumberland Review (USA), *Poetry Live, Poetry Review, The Times Literary Supplement, South, London Magazine, Aurora, Slipping Glimpses* (Poetry Book Society, 1985), *Tribune, Prospice, The Green Book Anthology, Voices* (Arts for Labour anthology, Pluto Press), *Write In* (Southern Arts), *Between the Lines, Poems at Hanover, Writing, P.E.N. Magazine, Orbis, Purple and Green* (33 Women Poets, Rivelin Grapheme), *Consequences.*

'Spanish Moss' was first published as a *Headland 'Poetry Live' Poemcard*

HAND TO MOUTH

The man on the corner is selling carnations,
roses and flowers I cannot even name,
for I do not enter florist's shops,
hotel foyers or help to light the flame
which begins suburban barbecues.

The loaded barrow he owns I recognise at once,
and understand the long haul to some back street.
Later, there is a stall selling hot pies,
hamburgers and tea, but I am afraid to eat,
hand to mouth, and hurry past.

How did they trudge away slowly that year
from the piles of rotting potatoes, the smell,
the baby riding on her father's shoulders,
clutching his thick hair, the one who fell
by the way, dead of road fever?

She was only eight years old, my grandmother,
and England hostile to a long-faced Celt.
When she lost her Irish name she rather
fancied her new English one, and felt
proud of her six book-learning children.

IN THE LYRICAL TRADITION

That I loved you in the best traditions
of lyrical poetry, which is where I began,
will never be remembered. Invisible
to the naked eye, the microscopic dots
form themselves into sexual fantasies.
The ear cannot hear them, nor is there
the slightest hint of salt on the tongue,
and sensations from the finger-tips
show only in the faintest trembling
of a hand on a page, writing.

Over-sensitive, touchy and thin-skinned,
I am yet the joker in the pack,
throw double sixes, climb patiently up
ladders, fall down snakes, begin again.
I prize open my diaries' brass clasps,
break a nail, a heart, rummage about
for passion, sex and art, which I
had packed away for good, and find
this lyrical poem, asking to be made,
written by a hand on a page, trembling.

EGO TRIP

All you brought with you was your face,
and the keeping of a promise, two books
and that invisible companion, Super Ego,
sitting beside you in the driver's seat,
poor Libido locked like a prisoner,
or a body in the boot.

I hope never again to feel the cold
unwilling touch and the dutiful kiss.
Kind Uncle Alter Ego, who really just
came along for the ride, encouraged
you from the back seat, but cunningly
moved local landmarks.

You lost your way, confused and turning
into the wrong minor roads. No one knew
if Id was there, although he could have
been crouched in the tissue pocket,
wiping his eyes like a sad marsupial,
crying by instinct.

SMALL DOLE

I should have been warned.
You laugh too much and Latin
quips multiply like fleas
in doss-house beds.

You are on the outside looking in.
I am the one who really saw
the dead on the floor,
laboured too long over
poems and lost causes.

I knew by your house that you were not
my kind, and never would be,
although you were caring and good
in the ways of the gentry,
a little patronising,
although not meaning to be.

You remind me of the ones
who worked my mother to death
and gave us clothes and smiles
and praised our hair, for theirs
was thin. Could servant's children
really have a thing called
a crowning glory?

Too late I saw I had come
up from the basement, knocked
at the wrong door, muddled
my grammar, been too much
above myself.

Brother or patron, rival or friend,
we were not the same, you and I.
Dole money is what it says.
The hungry thirties are there
for you to see in my face.

TOO MUCH ANGST

Too much angst, the young sculptor says,
showing me two copulating bicycles
welded in brass and the size of a hand.
Maybe, like us, they are just attached
to each other in a friendly way.
He says it's just a one-line joke,
queues up for dole money,
helps himself to coke.

I knock off sculpted icicles from gutters
in a careless way, he solders on a laughing fish,
detached and laid back as he stutters.
He plans an exhibition sometime in May.
I play around with words in the way
I do, dealing out my grimy pack of inhibitions.
He adds some floating sea-weed and a trident.
I add that touch of angst with words
he doesn't care for, brash and strident.

We don't do much good, but don't do too much harm.
He's waiting for his life to start,
I'm wondering if my fibrillating heart
means anything, but I'm laughing and he's calm.
The coupling bicycles ride off arm in arm.

MUNICIPAL IKEBANA

Only a small island; smaller since you left,
this drab cold spring of snowdrops under snow
and out-of-season chrysanthemums on your grave.
You had no choice but to bend your ear
to the platitudes of others and rinse away
my kisses from your mouth, inserting the gag
of commonplace acceptance and put on the face
they wanted, throwing out the whisky cache
hidden behind the solid rows of books.

Only a short time; shorter since you went away,
this snow and sun backdrop with a last sequence
of poems clothed in grey and unsigned this time,
taking up only a sliver of space on the shelf
beside by bed. All the techniques of survival
have been packed away and turned into obituaries
which got it wrong but cannot now apologize.
Let me, like you, not go down mealy-mouthed
at the last, or making promises I cannot keep.

Only a brief gesture; briefer since you fled
this resurrection time of municipal cherry
branches stashed in wine carafes everywhere,
stolen ikebanas instead of wilting wreaths.
I search among my tights for black ones
with no holes, but find only red. So. It is done.
I always could be relied upon to let you down
in public, my cold fists clenched in my pockets
like a threat, like a first signal of revolution.

EARLY SORROW

After the big blow they came
to clear the garden — the strong
good-looking boys, whose names
are Adam, shall we say, or Tom,
the little girl whose hair is long.

We'll christen her Chloe, or maybe,
later on, Emma, or even Jane.
We have to learn how they see
the toppled trees, the torn-up roots,
the sparkling splinters of the cold-frame.

Perhaps they are too young to be
aware of the connotations I need
to give this scene and if these three
will seem credible or how these plants
broadcast such appalling seeds.

This early sorrow may send one
child searching. They may go
to remote countries — Adam or Tom,
or even Chloe, but not Jane
or Emma, who will not even know

that they had rather outré names,
and had to go, so badly cast
for enduring the real war games
reserved for all these children
feeding bonfires on the edge of holocaust.

At the end of the day they came
into the house, had tea by lamplight,
dried their wet socks. Their names
are Anton, shall we say, or Heinz,
and little Irina laughing with delight.

The ash settles, the night is still,
a litter of branches covers the lawn,
urban foxes come silently to kill.
In Amarillo, USA, the white train
shudders along the rails at dawn.

ALPHABET BOARD

We sit out in the sun,
the patients and the staff,
wheel-chairs nuzzling
each other, the fountain
plashing gently,
like a romantic film.

Robin's alphabet board
lies on the courtyard;
his moving toe
picks out letters
with a mauve uncertainty
as we wait.

I. W.A.N.T. we follow
with our screwed-up eyes,
paralysed only with heat,
T.O. T.A.L.K.
We nod; the trees
shudder a natural palsy.

DE PROFUNDIS

At the centre of the stage
she commands them to be happy.
Positive thinking she calls it,
urging them on like an evangelist.
She produces Alice in Wonderland
in wheel chairs, encouraging the Mad Hatter
into further madness, the dormouse
into a deeper sleep. Afterwards
she tenderly wipes bottoms, lifts them
into bed, shows them her snapshots
of Zimbabwe, kisses them goodnight.

A negative thinker all my life, I am
waiting in the wings. They cry for me,
and swear blind they're getting worse,
pull out catheters or fall out of bed.
Suddenly, even the little speech
they had deserts them, they twitch
and break their finger splints.
Writing for me they become miniature
Ibsens, Norwegian to their finger-tips,
inhabit gloomy houses by cold seas,
learn the patter of Berryman, freak out.

I am only the writer in residence.
She re-writes their fragile histories
into brave and funny art-work, new Thurbers,
passes from one to another easily
with her curly hair and bright African dress,
her large body and her large heart,
her everyone's mother's voice chiding.
Everyone's child, I hunch in corners,
waiting for my one-line part, alert
for despair and bitter railing against fate,
altering the score from Gloria to De Profundis.

YOU TOUCHED ME

Never practised necrophilia
although bloody nearly
when the Major died
four days afterwards.
Among the paras and the quads,
the neurological misfits,
the alcoholics and the shits
you were the only one
who touched me.
Touching us up
was part of the
grotesque world
of hopeless cases;
sixteen or sixty
didn't matter to them,
just the fantasy,
but you, with your
noble countenance
and your soft-spoken
innuendoes, suddenly
undid me, calling me
Sweetie like they did
in the movies.
It was crap
to get me to share
my own clapped-out longings
and worn-out flesh
but,
you touched me.

A PERILOUS ZONE

'I still find myself in a perilous zone' extract from a letter.

    He sits beside her. He comes
from a far country and does not yet
greet friends or say very much
with his few words of English
through his broken teeth,
his thin and hesitant smile.
He is, in fact, a grey person, exiled
in a strange land.
*God, what a winter we've had,
and the Spring late and deceitful.*

    He knows about deceit, as he knows
our words of welcome, and does not yet
trust our hand-shakes or our weather.
He withdraws himself every time
the airmail letters come,
wrapping himself in his great-coat
with the high fur collar,
drinking vodka in the bar
and looking over his shoulder.
In a strait-jacket how can I do semaphore?

    She sits beside him. She has a husband
but left him behind in the provinces.
For him she has altered her hair,
learned to cook the dishes of his homeland.
He has crossed many frontiers
to perfect the look of her in clothes
of a more exotic kind than ours.
He faces East in bed and she lies
with her face to the West from habit.
*Close the curtains. I feel that the moon
has a watchful face and a cruel look.*

She knows about love as she knows
about the censored letters and the dim lights
of Blue Ward, where the far countries
of the mind parted them with no identity papers.
Unscrambling word-salads they come
to this newly built terminal,
trying not to look afraid at the barrier.
They have waited for so long and now
can hardly recognize each other.
I have hidden my notebooks in the garden.
The hole is marked with a green stick.

AN IDEAL FAMILY

They come running through the lighted dark,
a good bunch of kids from a comfortable wife.
In the broad lap of his chair he sees them
propping him up like the cushions of his life.

As they home back, his pigeons to the loft,
he thinks of the one in the shallow grave,
the uncomfortable woman and her haggard looks
of love and her unattainable secret cave.

Celebrating, as they do so often, the ideal family
are toasting the perfection of their illusions,
and eating well in the conventional manner
he has trained them to — the master of delusions.

They come running through the darkening light,
carrying in their hands the prisoner's grain,
and the sound of their unclipped wings dies away
as he welcomes them all back home again.

LETTING GO

I've always liked those grand exits;
the audience in tears, the critics
muted for once, the opera house stage
littered with final bouquets of roses.

Yet, isn't it better to just disappear,
the phone calls and letters unanswered,
letting go, and backing out quietly,
scrawling *not known at this address.*

Whoever paints the walls in this room,
(and, My God, they need some colour),
should never know what went on in here,
and be grateful walls don't have ears.

Well, must close now, my father used
to write, as if locking up the shop
was a kind of rehearsal for a final appearance,
easing a muslin shroud over bacon pieces.

I've outstayed my welcome in this house,
and must pack my luggage for the journey —
some dope, some booze, a handkerchief
and a parcel of easily erased memories.

I never liked sad endings; the long walk
into the lurid sunset, FIN blotting out
the last warmth, so why do I lovingly
edit sub-titles for this silent movie?

A STRAW MAT

I am guilty, she said to me. I didn't know what to say.
We are all guilty, I said, of something, if it's only living

when turf rests heavy on all the people cut off in their prime,
or buying this old cardigan from Oxfam instead of doing

something real. She said, Like what? I didn't know.
I saw my tears fall on the leper's foot. What a nonsense.

Africa is thirsty for blood and yet more blood, and we
wander round the Oxfam shop, thinking that woven mat

will do for the bit of the kitchen floor the cats leave
lion paw-prints on. *Please, I beg you, do not.* Scream.

I will and can. Blood and fear and no, no mercy
up in the top field where the bodies lie bludgeoned

and raped and still, their heads turned away, into the grass,
their legs still apart, the screams still forming on their lips.

Somewhere, someone said, That'll do for Oxfam, and we saunter
past the shelves of clothes, a queer smell in our nostrils,

like guilt, like spilt sperm, like reparation. We teeter
on the edge of a communal grave, clutching a straw mat and 10p.

TEA WITH COPERNICUS AND WAFFLES

(for Nicki and Andrzej)

In the goldfish bowl which grew
into a tower as the afternoon sun
ran up the steep hill to the ranks
of houses, the cat Abigail,
and the child too,
listened quietly to the words
which ran like mice over
the exercise book.

Sun-centred, the house went round
too fast. Good-bye, Mathematike syntaxis.
Nicolaus is lying on his bed.
You went mad, you said, buying
a king-size duvet for the double bed.
Cots, coffins, catafalques;
your shroud is really only
a motor-bike under a canvas cover.

How did she know that Mimi with flowers
would greet her from the armchair,
or that political pamphlets pushed
under doors would at last be picked up
by the right hands, the one with the pen,
the other with the brush, and the child
eating ice-cream on a June day,
the wind whipping over the town
where old mistresses come to die?

The waffles lay on the plates
like leaded panes on windows,
honey falling through the lattices,
tea warming the wiry suture
in her gum, as the midnight sky
floated above his bed, the cat,
Abigail, quitting her chair
and sitting quietly in the middle
of the canvas, as the child sat
between her parents and the visitor
with the bruise on her jaw.

Have you finished your French?
bring back the change.
Here is a woman pursued by a snake
as she looks through the bannisters.
Is it a snake or a rope?
And who is visiting who,
would you think?
Who is building a house
with words or paint?
Is it him? Is it her?

We are all honey catchers,
gatherers of peacock feathers,
peaceful winners of wars.

DRINKING WITH HENRY

There we were, the three of us,
wreathed in sea fog.
Laugh? I could have died.
You and I raked our skimpy purses
for money, shared a tonic,
laughed about his little legs,
ghostly gossips, sending up men,
but loving them, scrabbling up
from the pit once again
with our red boots,
our bottles of henna,
and our sticky buns and coffee.

There's nothing you can do
to keep him from letting you down.
It's not that we really
wanted his company,
but he's more constant
than the men you had —
a close companion,
you might say.

Nobody saw us come down the hill,
or looked twice at our pinched faces.
Waving goodbye, like lovers
or sisters, we felt that choking sense
of loss, the black bag over our heads.

Cats are all triangles, you said,
going back to the basket of knitting,
the lists of addresses,
and the signed paintings.
I hold out my hand
to stop myself from falling,
and see you talking
to your mirror, before he sliced you
in half, and left you for dead.

REDEMPTION

(i.m. H.S.)

Breathing comes as easy to me
as dreaming, fantasies come and go.
I live in another world from this.
Somewhere a man is gasping for air,
like a fish just landed on the shore.
This is another world again —
in, out, in out, in orgasmic fury,
a sour and lonely winding-in,
a gagging on terror, a taut line.

On the washed stones a thin
sprinkling of blood and the twitch
of unhooked silver bodies;
the boys scramble up the shingle,
taunting the girls behind the wall.
Hunter to prey they single
out the one who always cries
stinking fish, waving their hands
under her nose and laughing.

Sometime just before sunrise
the nurse comes round the ward,
with her mermaid's hair tucked
under her cap, another world
from the seas she sails upon
as she sleeps through the morning.
Breathing comes as easy to me
as dreaming. I am pawning
my heart for an oxygen mask
and a silver hip-flask,
with two chances to one
of redemption.

VERY SAMUEL

She says her cat is looking
very Samuel today.
Cats have very sideways
secret smiles, she says.
(Cats look very Samuel
when you cover their ears
with your hand.
Don't ask me why.)

Both of my cats are called
Pookiesnackenburger
for a few weeks, called
Desdemona and Othello
before that, and the vet
has them on his file
as Solomon and Salome.
(These are Biblical cats,
after a long line of
literary lads, ending with
Pushkin.)

After burying Pushkin
in a very Russian way,
with Myshkin peering
into the grave
like an idiot,
we walked away like cats,
pressing the balls
of our feet into the grass,
carrying our tails
for convenience.
(All across the Steppes
the howling echoed,
the kittens crouched
with their paws
tucked under, listening.)

Cats walk in and out
of poems, their secret worlds
as mysterious as ours.
I have just come out
of the long grass,
acting tiger.
She has seen a notice saying
GOOD HOMES WANTED
FOR KITTENS.
(Soon there will be
more cats than people,
with our hands over their
pointed lovely ears.
Don't ask me why.)

FORM

'I own a quarter of a racehorse' — ERNIE SMITH

The horse of Dr. Syntax has come in
long after Jade Lady and Grand Parade;
Grizzle is galloping riderless, all skin
and bone. Phallus has made Heraclius
a happy man and Phrenicos has just won
the 73rd Olympiad, and My God, here come
the four horsemen of the Apocalypse.
Neck or nothing, double or quits,
the stakes are higher now, the Turf
a lyrical world, a string of names.
An odd-ball, gesticulating this divot poetry —
Dead Beat, Five Alive, Blonde Beauty,
Perou, Red Light, Back Seat, Bounden Duty,
he wears his red and white colours,
Bradford boy.

ASSAULT AND BATTERY

What's he in for?
Assault and battery.
Some really punchy poems
on violence I think.

But no, the roses are pink,
there's a cottage door,
and the clouds are smaller
than a man's hand.

His paintings are bland
the art teacher says.
The cottage is there too,
and a phalanx of flowers.

Excitement grows. He is ours.
The painter and I glow
with ideas of a country
childhood somewhere.

He was reared, but where?
A slum in Hull, or Hell
or Halifax? He doesn't
quite know. Wrong again.

The shrink smiles with pain,
remembering a fragment
in the dig of therapy;
some faded floral wallpaper.

Well, we knew a taper
of truth would be significant,
and this is where his dad
duffed up his mum one day.

No, he didn't say,
but every time he'd watched
for isolated cottages
and women living alone.

Men don't bring roses home;
they plant them on women,
burn buds with ciggy ends
to keep the garden growing.

Goodnight. We're going.
He makes the screws really sick
to the stomach. They'd like
to kick his head in after classes.

Him and his bloody roses.

THE JOKE SHOP

The chattering joke teeth, the cigar
exploding, is a minor torment.
Better this way than watching
the prisoners jump from shocks.
Your wife is standard, but the
magnetic lady in the bath
is only three inches long.
Have fun with whoop-ee cushions
and empty the bar with stink bombs.
It's better than the real thing:
buying realistic severed fingers
and bloody bandages keeps life
at bay as well as death.
The talking toilet tells us all
cowering against the bathroom wall.

THIS ROOM

'We can't really spend our whole life in this room.'
FRANCOISE SAGAN.

Since you took me by the hand
and led me to my mother's unmade bed,
I have never got it right with men.
I remember the pale sun lighting up
the flowered wallpaper, the counterpane.

I had played doctors and nurses
in the shadowed back yard many times,
but did not think to play it with you,
although at first you were a kind doctor
and told me what I had to do.

Doing the Miserere on London Bridge
with a man who wore your thick hair
and your name and had a way with words,
I begged for forgiveness, plucking at
my nurse's badge among the crowds.

This surreal scene of secret games
is my hall-mark and my contredanse,
and persuades me to bare white walls,
broken marriages and dubious friendships,
the crying voices asking me to call.

Since you took me by the hand
and led me to my mother's unmade bed,
I have waited to be shown this cell,
the healing physicians opening up wounds,
guiding me to the peep-hole into hell.

THE BRADFORD CONNECTION

(for Philip Callow)

I have been incommunicado
since I threw the gelded tree away
and looked at the unsuitable gifts —
soap on a rope, a book to look at,
a mainstream poet's collected work,
all manacled together with rhymes
and family relationships.
Christmas is when the cracks show.

I came to Bradford alone,
lying in that hotel room, curled up
in my black tights to keep
the cold away, and other things;
the TV on the wall, the old dog
playing in the yard with a ball
like an abandoned foetus,
trailing entrails everywhere.

I went to Lister Park and trod
on the long red tongue hanging
over the gallery floor. I nearly
fell on my ass, the floors were
so highly polished and Emily
under glass with her sisters,
the old books, the documents
in faded laborious copperplate.

I meant to write and say
that it's better to keep away
from my terrible dark rooms,
my artful clichés and my disrespect
for the language of flowers and hedges,
my love of gaunt and tatty cities.
My cats are like beautiful inbred girls;
they wear brown suede boots.

They sit in the lighted windows
wearing their natural make-up
and their fur coats which are
a perfect fit, watching the men go by,
the tips of their tails interlaced.
Strangely, they are as timid as I am,
their eyes shine deep red at night,
the moon silvers their fur.

A TRANSLATION

'I was a man from Japan who met you at the poetry reading.
Do you remind of it?'

From the safe harbour of the man
with her father's name she darted
into the open sea, a small fish alive
among the sharks and smiling dolphins.
No shingle of gentility dragged
at her ankles as she arranged
the red blouse over her pregnant body
and left behind the people wailing
on the shore for medicines and love.
Only the waves queued up patiently
with white faces; passing ships
called for life-belts and bandages,
but she swam on into deeper waters,
the scarlet dye marking her progress
like a graph of feeling rising
sharply. The coastlines faintly
sketched their last pencil markings
on the horizon like a Japanese
translation of her English name,
the poem which flew to Tokyo.

Yes, Takao, I remind of it.

THE NOVELIST

Having lovers was not
what she expected.
It made for a lot
of planning
and a great deal
of anguish.

They never got
to the essence of her,
and left her to rot
after a few years
of getting written up
unkindly.

The cats were not
a great help either,
or the pot
under the bed,
and cigarette smoke
in her hair.

Having her was not
what they expected.
It made for a lot
of effort
and not enough
of the other.

They were off like a shot
as soon as she started
ignoring the plot
and leaving out
their tender sensitive
natures.

EDWARD THOMAS AT SURINDERS

(Surinders: a cafe in West London which has poetry readings)

Why am I sitting here?
I left the maps and my pipe
and my last letter to Helen
somewhere between the battle-line
and that cold new house
where the child sickened
and the joists were new.

Why didn't you bring us all?
Lorenzo would have been
at home persuading Frieda
to wear her Bavarian outfit,
but what would we have done
with Rilke tugging
at Leishman's hand?

What are these influences?
After all, you would never
follow me on those lonely walks,
your shoes highly unsuitable
and your sense of direction
ruining any compass
I might give you.

I only borrowed your voice
for a while, Edward, preferring
to play Eurydice at the pit-head.
Betteshanger is everywhere,
I find, silent in the snow.
I hew at my seam of words
in the only way I know.

MODEL T.

Mr and Mrs Karl Marx
are having a picnic
on Chalk Hill.
Toy bears are going blind
and the Model T is still
sliding backwards.

The three children
of Mr and Mrs Karl Marx
who are dead
cannot come back and ride
on their father's back
but lie down instead.

In Soho the two rooms
are full of words,
which Mr and Mrs Karl Marx
encourage like caged birds
practising the notes
of a new anarchy.

The other children
who are underfed, but alive
play with their toys,
but Mr and Mrs Karl Marx
don't mind the games
and the noise.

Engels is finding his way
through the tobacco smoke
and stubbing his toe
on broken furniture owned
by Mr and Mrs Karl Marx,
used by Qui-Qui and Quo-Quo.

They are learning the lines
which send away
the debt-collectors who
do not see the red flag fly,
or visit the graves
of Mr and Mrs Karl Marx

when they die.

A GENETIC ERROR

This is the screaming baby, arching
his back with wind, oddly dressed
in his girl's smocked nightgown,
addicted to gripe-water, rehearsed
star of their melancholy inbred world
the negative answer to their searching.

His genes have drawn the wrong number
in the raffle of life — too many noughts
to win the prize and carry it away.
All the toyshops where they bought
his pleasures and amusements closed down
like Oxfam's riffled-through December.

This is the listening mother, writing
down his history of shrinking options,
like a character in an Ibsen play,
filling in forms for fictional adoptions,
paying her dues to foster parents
who soon tire of sick in-fighting.

There is nowhere he can safely go,
this full-grown child, except to sleep
in unmade beds in damp basement rooms,
waking suddenly at night to keep
the living wake of the walking dead,
joining the sleepers down below.

IRISH HAIR

Coming over from Ireland, the boat
lurching its way in snapping wind,
the decks wet and slippery with spume,
the girl, Christiana Breary,
is leaving behind the stench
of rotting potatoes, the abandoned
household goods, the shallow trench
where they left her brother
wrapped hastily in straw,
the baby dead of road fever,
seeming at the last to cry
bread or blood, and then silence.

She is nearly six years old.
When she was four it was
a fine hot summer until August
rain and biting sleet
wetted her bare feet.
She does not know that the boat
will dock at Liverpool and not Quebec,
that they will throw her mother
into the sea, free from the misty confusion
of typhus, free from the unfounded illusion
of a better life. She does not know
that she will marry into pure Norman stock,
a man gaunt as a gibbet, melancholy
as an undertaker, and that from her
will be extracted a life of labour,
but not smell of famine or abandoning
of home and children.

They brought with them the two
brass candlesticks, wrapped
in a camisole and a pair of corsets,
the youngest riding on his shoulder.
Her father will find a new wife,
now scrubbing steps in Watling Street,
the roads the Romans made, as he
will make English roads with his pick.
She is tired of serving the gentry,
but not crying of the hunger,
the basement kitchen warmed
by well-stoked ovens.

Buying my bag of potatoes I hurry
to the hairdressers. Cutting
my coarse hair the girl says :
'We call this Irish hair',
and nearly a century later I now
think of her, Christiana Breary,
my father's mother, who made
her own pilgrim's progress
to an alien land, her bible in her hand,
and in her body her unseen corn seed
which will never exorcise the devil
of hunger, or my own anger.

MRS DESECRATE'S BABY BOY

When it came at last
it was a bouncing baby boy.
Holding this bloody object
by the heels as she smacked it
into life, the midwife asked :
What are you going to call him,
Sacred or Profane?

Profane, said Mrs Desecrate,
who bore this false child
too late, and my, it was a mongol.
They were very loving children,
the midwife said, and wiped
his bottom as the mother
wiped her eyes.

She had thought of names
like Precious, or Relationship,
(he was, after all, human,
if a little marred
by his slanting eyes).
Profane Desecrate, she said
and put her hand behind his head.

THE EIGHT-FOLD WAY

She is the one who sits looking gloomily out
across the school playing fields, perched
uneasily at a child's broken desk.
She's been this way before; it's just her legs
are longer now, school is in the evenings,
and she knows about all those sexual mysteries
whispered about in corridors and changing rooms.

She is not getting on too well
with the eight-fold way, or non-coursing,
and the concept of reality eludes her,
as the wheel goes slowly round.
Vaguely, and all her teachers told her
not to dream her time away, she thinks
perhaps the study of Zen Buddhism
was not quite right for her, but it gets her
away from the sullen house, the monosyllabic hours,
the toppling piles of books and manuscripts,
and nobody smokes, so the perpetual smell
of nicotine fades, and the old ash of chalk
falls on her sleeve.

She is naive, that's the trouble, and lonely too.
Her sex life is down to zero, and her looks have gone,
her talents questionable, and her thyroid
isn't functioning as it should, leaving her
always cold and forgetful and extremely tired.
The lecturer, in the zest of his fountains
of words despairs of her, languishing there
weekly; she doesn't get the point, drives him
spare when she remarks that Samsara is the name
of one of her Siamese cats.

She looks sometimes as if she might be meditating,
but he guesses she is thinking of things
he didn't put on his careful syllabus.
In the end, he thinks of her as a mark
on the register. She rarely speaks
and hardly appears to listen, and when he
loses his temper she just stares and smiles.
On the train home he is uneasy and troubled
by thoughts of her remote air, her quiet
presence, and sees her standing
in a saffron robe, thin from fasting,
shimmering in a heat haze, holding her
begging bowl. As he gets off
at his predetermined destination,
he is struck by the odd thought
that Nirvana is the name of his station.

IMAGO 1943

I am aware at last that once you go
there will be no one to remember me
in just that way, or say that snow
was not whiter than my skin, which no sun
ever browned, for there is no way to know
what kind of transformation happened
to such a gawky girl, before you came.
Such short years, the chrysalis time,
and you in your cavalry greatcoat name
me wife, with my tartan cloak and green
suede shoes, and no photographs to frame,
for I was virgo intacta, in camera, imago.

TRIPTYCH

1. Going to Tenby.

Moscow is always somewhere else, we said,
because we fancied we were Chekhov's people,
but why we thought this I can no longer remember.
The packed trunk in the hall, perhaps, was all
it really came to, or my mournful wanderings
through shuttered houses, picking up the sound
of sledges on snow, or long skirts brushing
the dust on varnished wooden verandah floors
in rented houses on the West coast of Wales.
Looking out to Caldey, the dead major's guns
slung on the wall, we could imitate them all,
listening for the axe strokes to begin for us,
packing to go to Dunwich with the children wailing,
and the cats sedated in their wicker baskets.

2. On Dunwich Beach.

In the end, I think, there is nothing for it
but to set out alone to Dunwich beach,
jerkily crossing the pallid sands, each foot-print
an erratic poem of heel and sole, heel and sole
to the end. This is where I would choose to go,
until I found the sea again, and never stop
when the waves gagged me and the sea-weed bound me
tight as loving arms. There are no family names
I wish to remember, except those inbred girls,
my aunts, Christiana, Edith, Joyce and Bessie,
who never did those dreadful genetic sums —
one into one makes three, or four, or more.
The children's plates are packed on the top,
and Charlotte is whispering to the sleepy cats.

3. Towards Ditchling Beacon.

It is a long time since you brought me here,
switching the car radio off, silencing a voice
in mid-sentence like a coronary moving through
the ether, that swift striker unseen among the players.
The Beacon will not dazzle in our headlights now,
or receive again the picnic blanket or the riders
of the night who meet me on the road with faces
from the past, the sly cats-eyes marking out
the miles as if we were bound with Ngugi* to Yalta.
I touch the petals of blood with timid fingers
as we make this journey backwards into births
and wars, remembering the delicate profiles
turned towards us as I pull on the family face
and we carry cats and children into the empty house.

* Ngugi Wa Thiong'o finished his novel *Petals of Blood* in Yalta.

FIGHT OR FLIGHT

His muted talent hovers
on the edge of boredom,
his stilted letters leave out
the horrors and the failures.
He pats himself on the back
for being so restrained,
fastens his newly-ironed shirt
and covers the buttons
with his tastefully modest tie.
He tells her she looks nice,
as if she might be a meal,
a garden, a sweet
or a church candle.
She flails around angrily,
her laddered black stockings
hiding the knotted veins,
and her distressed leather
hiding her distressed heart,
but exhibiting her feelings
in black and red — this year's
colours, her sixty years
flaunting the pavements
as her impatient heels
clack in art galleries
without him. Like trapped
animals they demonstrate
the theory of fight or flight.

FROM THIS DAY ON

'From this day on painting is dead.' — DE LA ROCHE.

These radiant draped dolls
who loll in perfection before
the camera, will follow the hearse
of painting, rehearsing their faces.
Click. Click. You're dead.
They are holding the wake of art
in the Grand Salon of Paris;
the mourners are in black and white,
startled and bleached by the flash gun,
or cropped off by clumsy amateurs
as they linger by the door.

The empty house, the car parks,
the deserted street corners
are waiting for the silent murderers
to come in a blur of red,
the nudes are getting colder every minute.
Diane Arbus is recording the edges
of bleak lives and arranging
her own death somewhere behind
closed shutters on the way
to U.S. Highway 285
with her black box in her hand.

The photographer's wife
is rarely caught in the act,
retreating from lush landscapes
and faint markings of lost villages
in colours she is not aware of.
She crosses his soaring bridges
when she comes to them, for the river
is his monochrome, and hers too.
They link steel hands rigidly
over waters deeper than they know —
not Pont du Gard, but Battersea.

SOLOMON'S SEAL

When you first gave me
the dried roots, the limp leaves,
I did not think to see
the little dangling flowers
this year, green and white,
subdued prisoners hung
for innocent crimes
under the swarthy green
of oppressive leaves.

The Requiem Mass
for dead tulips is over.
the fierce blue stars
of forget-me-nots fading
like the painted statue
I kept the first year
of our marriage, Our Lady
of the Five Wounds fighting
with the Queen's Proctor
for my immortal soul.

No confessional curtain
took me from you,
 and no stitched-on yellow star
took you from me.
The clematis is doing
a crucifixion against the wall,
our vine has tender grapes.
All winter the snow
kept iron guards
in every corner.

READING IN CAMBRIDGE

I brought you here, a day
in late May, the doctor tired,
the gas and air turning the bed
into a sailing ship, nurses
into lanterns. I bled you out
to a hostile world, harsher
than the arid places
I had just travelled from,
with my faulty poems
and my Janus faces

I left you here, a day
in early June, the poems read,
the cycles gathered together
under NO CYCLES, New Square
enclosing the brief grass,
ignoring your timid prayer.
Addenbrooks, the brutal guardian
of the fens, raised a shout
of warning as the train
sidled through the dampening air.

I found you here, a day
in mid-July, the tablets scattered
on the floor, the sirens wailing,
the thesis papers scored
with lines, the windows pasted
over, the notice-board
empty: a near-death to call
me back with my fee clutched
in my hand, exacting your own dues,
and trailing your withered cord.

NUDE DECLINING

Bible-backed and stiff after Yoga classes
she is no Venus Anadyomene, but perhaps
was once the Venus Genetrix to her husband
and the Venus Callipyge to her lover.
Watering her maidenhair ferns alone
she remembers collapsed blancmanges
like her own heavy flesh, white puddings,
and her mother's corsets a hanging pink armour,
partnered by her father's truss, the deep bed
where a broken feather in the wing pricked
her to sleep after all those childhood sicknesses.

Meadow saffron is blooming all the year
as she washes carefully each day at those
blurred outlines, unwilling to dress herself
in dishonest clothes, defenceless and exposed
as a stony caryatid holding up a city
without men, her aching arms too thin by half.
The zinc bath no longer hangs on the door,
no corsets and trusses loop the brass bed knobs.
Turning the world upside down she sleeps
under the duvet, her leotard empty on the floor —

a nude declining.

SMILE FOR DADDY

At last he is quiet; his harsh words
can no longer scare the living daylights
out of me. I never understood the story
they told me of him in hospital asking
to see me, dressed in my new brown coat,
aged three or four. To-day I wear my black.
Bartletts as far as the eye can see pack
the crematorium pews. Don't nick the books
of Common Prayer, the gilded lettering pleads.
He would have liked to see us all walking
in the rain behind a gun-carriage, his medals
lying on the polished coffin lid,
a sort of mini state funeral, the slow drums,
the tolling bells, the black veils.

He fought, but did not bleed or die
for his country, as he disciplined
but did not love his children.
Smile for Daddy. Somewhere there's a face
grimacing at a window, a small girl held high
in the air, a pale hand waving weakly.
All the men I've loved knock on wood,
and seem to wear his humourless stare,
used me for bayonet practice, went absent
without leave, could reduce me to tears,
as he did, but they were not aware
of this, and so we wait for him to disappear,
silenced at last, although not in my dreams,
but that is my funeral, not his.

THIN ICE

Though it was a thing of the past,
the snow stayed all summer long.
Condemned without trial or jury
she walked, pinch-faced, while others
oiled their lover's backs on hot
beaches, sucked lollies, undid bras.

No one provoked him with impunity,
this Jack-in-the-green, but skating
over thin ice she was so light
the tourists took her photograph
back to the U.S. of A. and Paris,
passing through the customs with ease.

Back in Utah they pored over polaroids
and though they were proud of Stratford,
Hampton Court and Morris dancers' hats,
they could not explain this ice lady,
the freakish whiteness among the brown
arms and legs, the shorts and cans of beer.

The reference to Villon evaded them
and spoiled the effect of having done
England in one week. With secretive haste
many destroyed the black and white negative
among the colour prints, ashamed to show
their friends something so inexplicable.

In Bee-country, the new Jerusalem,
they did not wish to be a laughing stock,
remembering Carthage jail in Illinois.
Deseret was purged of gliding girls
from a foreign country with odder customs
than their own. They wiped away the frost.

BAROQUE NIGHTS AND NATURALISTIC DAYS

Acquainted with baroque nights
I am not impregnated with the smell
of poverty; not my skin or my clothes.
I am a neutral and unarmed observer
making my check calls, inserting smiles
into gaping mouths and looking for signs
of leaking roofs and naturalistic happenings,
like a dead bird on the floor of a cage,
or porno-collages on dusty walls.

Acquainted with naturalistic happenings
I am dusted all over with a pollen of light
and riches of hyacinths; my skin and my clothes.
I am armed with a blade of hart's tongue,
threadbare histories rest on my time-sheet.
They have tiled over the hole where the sky
looked through, and all the baroque nights
fly away like bats in the half-light,
making murals of fantasies on bright walls.

MR ZWEIGENTHAL

He was your other father, she said,
awkwardly. I was lucky to have
two fathers, I thought, but he was
a secret; left behind a bow-tie
like a black malevolent butterfly,
a looped violin string, an address
in Danzig, a baby in her bed.

Played beautiful he did, at the end
of the pier, the August sun dipping
slowly into the sea, the turnstile
creaking as they ran home, laughing,
sliding on shingle, clutching stones
and shells, but careful with his fiddle
and the black suit she used to mend.

What did he think, I asked, my real dad,
when he came home from India and found me
sleeping in the crib beside her?
Wasn't he pleased? Her face grew
cracked all over. The lodger, a Jew,
it wasn't meant . . . a mistake, the pills
didn't work. I felt so bad, so bad.

Mr Zweigenthal, I have your nose,
your hands, but no talent for a waltz,
a barcarolle. I know you almost as well
as I know myself, with your dark moods,
and your tall stooping figure which broods
over my whole life, looking out across
the Baltic, and in your buttonhole a rose.

GOODSFIELD (after Palmer)

Haymaking by moonlight, the stooks glow,
no longer golden, but drenched in red.

The pale people, sleeves rolled up, skirts
hitched, seem frozen in working attitudes.

It is the stooks which appear to move,
dancing two by two, so slowly it seems

hallucinatory under the little blind white
stars. The stone cider jar is passed round,

faces flush, one sheaf leans drunkenly
against another, mice in the ruined field

carry no fighting slogans like 'We were here
in the wheat ears, our quiet summer's residence

is gone.' The short stiff growth of stubble
is a dwarfed army, uneven, rigid and brittle,

a cloud passes over the moon, hiding her scars,
the laughter seeps away like stealthy blood,

the farm hands wipe their roughened hands
on furrowed corduroy and gathered skirts.

All this is gone now. Neat bound parcels
drop like swaddled babies on a prairie,

burnt fields turn black faces blankly away,
beer cans gleam in the dark corners, hedges

have gone, but seed is sown in the same tied
cottages, mothers pace on moonlit floors.

THEATRE IN THE ROUND

You were a cowardly lover, leaping dancer,
a swarthy Slav coming home after hunting,
walking more slowly as the clouds grew denser.
They roasted the pig and hung up the bunting,
but you were a yellow belly and your eyes
flickered in and out of focus, cognoscente
of failures and presidential fall-out shelters,
as they erected the swing-boats and helter-skelters.

Drifting through Soho where the clothes are scanty
and the blue movies asked you out to tea,
you never spared a caring thought for me,
crouched over the gas fire in red satin panties,
wearing my old dancing shoes, eight months gone.
Since we made our pas de deux I am all alone
except for the smallest member of the school
for contemporary dance, cavorting in his waters,
ready to spring naked from the wings.

I am a dressing room. I am theatre in the round.
You were my choreographer, drenched my feet
with french chalk, and my unprotected womb
with sperm, braced on your elbows, panting
into my neck. I've stuffed your letters
in the drawer with my leotards, pointing
my toes, and think of you walking in the streets
like a figure strayed into an abstract painting.

PER FUMUM

Sometimes I think of your novels in the loft.
The pages are all edged with brown now;
the characters smell of dust.

I think I hear Jordan talking to Dora.
He is giving her a bottle of Californian Poppy
for her birthday, and another child.

She is pulling Patrick up Lewes High Street
on a tin tray over the new snow;
the sky is gravid over the castle.

Your typewriter is clacking in Welsh,
banging in those terrible high rooms
where the mongol children laughed.

I am combing out my hair rather slowly
and awkwardly opening my legs
to a young midwife, and we are both afraid.

We are really like people in a novel,
writing up our lives in poems and journals
and piling up cairns of words.

Inside the cairns we are playing house
with dolly's cups and dolly's pork chops
and unbreakable pink blancmange.

You wrote about a baby wrapped in a parcel
after delivery. There are babies
in the loft who won't stop crying.

I roll the agent's notes and rejection slips
into ear-plugs and think idly about
nights in the gardens of Spain.

The midwife says 'Another boy, I'm afraid'.
I roll over and reach for my notebook
and my leaky fountain pen.

One day we must clear out the loft,
and go behind the hawthorn hedge
for the ritual burning of the books.

I think the snow will be scented like Dora,
but Patrick abandoned the painted tray
for me to paint new patterns on.

SPANISH MOSS

Long trails of Spanish moss hang
from the oak trees, dead hands
from the underworld.
In the drizzle faint cries of hounds,
great angular blocks of stone,
fresh-quarried, veins of marble, white
like the legs of a woman, sandstone
shaling to slate, the bones
of your land, the walls of buildings,
the facing of banks, the scarp
of combes.

Clitters of rock are as intractable
as people, mottled and obstinate
as the one you left behind,
sleeping sprawled under
a wild-flower quilt, stirring
alone under the fabric
of trendy daisies.

Rushes wind-lashed, and rain-sodden
you trample through; not like these mats
your wife walks softly on when she wakes,
searching for a sheet of paper
under a stone paper-weight.

THE CAVE YOU WOULD NOT ENTER

The cave you would not enter
was familiar to you, the frill
of sea-weed round the entrance,
the high cliffs above, and even
the obligatory screaming gull
inside my head. Sea-anemones
with their delicate-tongued
fellatio were the only flowers
to hold you over all the seas
of omission and commission.

Now, the speculum has explored
the cave with an eye as cold
and unwinking as your own,
instruments have scraped away
the limpets and the viscid walls
are waiting for the visitor
who never comes, or ever will
while there are mermaids to sing
sweeter songs than this bed
allows. Storm cones are hoisted
to warn sailors that these red
waters signify danger. I turn
and turn, riding out the storm
of fever and the drag of tides.

As the faint port-holed dawn
alerts this ancient liner
to another hospital day,
the wrecker's coastline
well to leeward in the centre,
I stop up with tampons
the cave you would not enter.

KIM'S GAME

She ran up and down the wet streets
peering myopically into empty alleys,
fingering dhotis which looked like his,
scrabbling round the wheels of panic
like a manic gerbil restless in a cage.
Everything looked like abandoned bazaars,
the troopers drawn out, the natives baffled
by the counter-commands of Creighton Sahib,
the quick and brutal curfew of silence.
Lutuf Ullah is gone to Kurdistan was scratched
on doors and walls. Impatient bastard,
she thought; he couldn't wait to go back
to the house with painted shutters,
the forbidden temple, the lines of words,
and the Amritsar girl turned on her side, asleep.
His disappearing act was just a return to base,
before the midnight pass ran out, and she
was only a messenger passing between the lines
with riddles for polis-Sahib, couched
in a highly emotional language, saying:
Much sorrowful delay. Rattling his sabre
he forced her to her knees and took away
her idiotic cyphers, her child's tray of toys
which she could never remember. The stallion
gallops to the North West Frontier; her father
is writing from Rawlpindi and she is not born.
She tries to think why men leave her, but all
that echoes round her mind are painted words:

Lutuf Ullah is gone to Kurdistan.

THE NUCLEAR GIRLS

It has been the summer
of erotic shoulder-blades
and vulnerable necks.
Among the hobble skirts
and the ballet pumps
move the grey and black girls
with their hair on end,
as if witnessing a preview
of the burning of the world —
quiche with mushrooms.

The weather hasn't been too good
this year, but bare legs are brown,
hair has been put up
in a Madame Bonnard style,
ready for the bath.
There is something for everyone,
but nothing, it seems, for me.
I am an old man,
watching the cattle market,
eating my junk food noisily.

Decades of summers ago
I would have hoped for a glimpse
of an ankle, and never thought
there would be so much flesh
to feed my hungry eyes.
They take me to Flanders
for the day. The wars
are ghosted transparencies
of poppies and landing craft,
bully beef and hard tack.

Sitting in the sun, I think
that life has been a dream,
seen for a moment and then gone.
I would like to stroke and touch
these nuclear girls before they float
as ashes on the wind,
stripped of their crumpled skirts,
offered on the world's menu
as crepes suzette,
or crepes noirs.